AQA (A) GCSE
Religious Studies

Unit 4
Roman Catholicism: Ethics

GCSE
Revision
GUIDE

Sheila Butler

PHILIP ALLAN
UPDATES

Philip Allan Updates, an imprint of Hodder Education, an Hachette UK company, Market Place, Deddington, Oxfordshire OX15 0SE

Orders
Bookpoint Ltd, 130 Milton Park, Abingdon, Oxfordshire OX14 4SB
tel: 01235 827827
fax: 01235 400401
e-mail: uk.orders@bookpoint.co.uk
Lines are open 9.00 a.m.–5.00 p.m., Monday to Saturday, with a 24-hour message answering service. You can also order through the Philip Allan Updates website:
www.philipallan.co.uk

© Philip Allan Updates 2009
ISBN 978-0-340-98717-9
First printed 2009

Impression number   5   4   3
Year   2014

Illustrations: Jim Watson
Printed in Dubai

Environmental information
Hachette UK's policy is to use papers that are natural, renewable and recyclable products and made from wood grown in sustainable forests. The logging and manufacturing processes are expected to conform to the environmental regulations of the country of origin.

P01479

Contents

About this book

Revision is vital for success in your GCSE examination. No one can remember what they learned up to 2 years ago without a reminder. To be effective, revision must be planned. This book provides a carefully planned course of revision — here is how to use it.

The book	The route to success
Contents list	**Step 1** Check which topics you need to revise for your examination. Mark them clearly on the contents list and make sure you revise them.
Revision notes	**Step 2** Each section of the book gives you the facts you need to know for a topic. Read the notes carefully, and list the main points.
Key words	**Step 3** Key words are highlighted in the text and displayed in key word boxes. Learn them and their meanings. They must be used correctly in the examination.
Test yourself	**Step 4** A set of brief questions is given at the end of each section. Answer these to test how much you know. If you get one wrong, revise it again. You can try the questions before you start the topic to check what you know.
Examination questions	**Step 5** Examples of questions are given for you to practise. The more questions you practise, the better you will become at answering them.
Exam tips	**Step 6** The exam tips offer advice for achieving success. Read them and act on the advice when you answer the question.
Key word index	**Step 7** On p. 64 there is a list of all the key words and the pages on which they appear. Use this index to check whether you know all the key words. This will help you to decide what you need to look at again.

Command words

All examination questions include **command** or **action** words. These tell you what the examiner wants you to do. Here are two of the most common ones:

- **Describe** — requires detail. For example, you may be asked to describe the rite of marriage. Description does not require explanation.
- **Explain** — here the examiner is expecting you to show understanding by giving reasons. For example, you may be asked to explain Roman Catholic views on abortion.

The checklists and advice opposite will help you to prepare for the exam and to make sure you do justice to yourself on the day.

Do you know?

- The exam board setting your paper?

- How many papers you will be taking?

- The date, time and place of each paper?

- How long each paper will be?

- What the subject of each paper will be?

- What the paper will look like? Do you write your answer on the paper or in a separate booklet?

- How many questions you should answer?

- Whether there is a choice of questions?

- Whether any part of the paper is compulsory?

If you don't know the answer to any of these questions as the exam approaches — ask your teacher.

Revision rules

- Start early.

- Plan your time by making a timetable.

- Be realistic — don't try to do too much each night.

- Find somewhere quiet to work.

- Revise thoroughly including learning the set texts — reading on its own is not enough.

- Summarise your notes, make headings for each topic.

- Ask someone to test you.

- Try to answer some questions from old papers. Your teacher will help you.

If there is anything you don't understand — ask your teacher.

Be prepared

The night before the exam

- Complete your final revision.

- Check the time and place of your examination.

- Get your pens ready.

- Go to bed early and set the alarm clock.

On the examination day

- Don't rush.

- Double check the time and place of your exam and your equipment.

- Arrive early.

- Keep calm — breathe deeply.

- Be positive.

Examination tips

- Keep calm and concentrate.

- Read the paper through before you start to write.

- In Part B, decide which questions you are going to answer.

- Make sure you can do all parts of the questions you choose.

- Complete all the questions.

- Don't spend too long on one question at the expense of the others.

- Read each question carefully, then stick to the point and answer questions fully.

- Use all your time.

- Check your answers.

- Do your best.

Christian values

The Bible is a very important source of values for Roman Catholics. It forms the basis for Church practice and teachings, the Sacraments derive their authority from it, and ordinary Roman Catholics turn to it for guidance in everyday life.

The Ten Commandments (Exodus 20:1–17)

* Worship God only

* Do not disrespect God's name

* Keep the Lord's day holy

* Honour your parents
* Do not kill
* Do not commit adultery
* Do not steal
* Do not commit perjury
* Do not covet your neighbour's wife
* Do not covet your neighbour's goods

The Ten Commandments consist of ten rules by which Christians believe they should live. They are found in the Bible. The first three commandments set out what a Christian's relationship with God should be. They demand absolute loyalty and devotion, respect and time set aside for God. Christians should not treat possessions or other people (e.g. celebrities) as gods or let other concerns squeeze God out of their lives.

The other seven set out how Christians should behave towards other people, in both family and wider society. Their relationships should be governed by respect.

Jesus' summary of the Ten Commandments
Love God with all your heart
Love your neighbour as yourself

The Bible forms the basis for Church practice and teachings

Fotolia

 Case study

Paul

- Aged 29
- Married with two young children
- Professional footballer for Scorewell Utd
- Roman Catholic

It's not always easy for me to stay true to my beliefs. I try to get to Mass every week and fit it in around travelling to and playing in matches. I find it very hard to love my neighbour when some people shout racist comments from the terraces. But God helps me not to lose my temper. The other lads go clubbing after the match and sometimes go off with girls they meet, but I think of my wife and children, so stay in my hotel room.

The Beatitudes (Matthew 5:1–12)

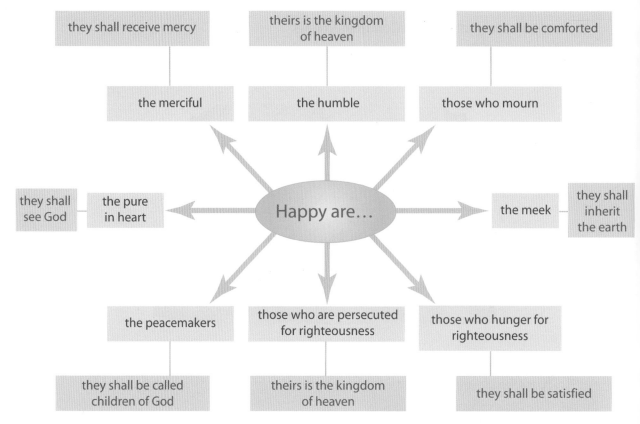

they shall receive mercy	theirs is the kingdom of heaven	they shall be comforted
the merciful	the humble	those who mourn

Happy are…

they shall see God — the pure in heart

the meek — they shall inherit the earth

the peacemakers	those who are persecuted for righteousness	those who hunger for righteousness
they shall be called children of God	theirs is the kingdom of heaven	they shall be satisfied

The word 'Beatitude' means 'happy' or 'blessed'. **The Beatitudes** are found in the Bible, in the section of St Matthew's Gospel that is known as the Sermon on the Mount. They are eight statements made by Jesus, and they list the qualities that Jesus thought people needed if they were to be truly happy, i.e. have a good relationship with God.

In today's world, as in the time of Jesus, those who get on in life are the pushy, those who fight tooth and nail for what they want, those with mixed motives, those always prepared to compromise, etc. Those who put others first, who are prepared to take a back seat and who are more concerned with what is right than what is in their best interests, are often despised. Jesus showed by example the kind of life he wanted his followers to live: he came to earth 'not to be served but to serve, and to give his life a ransom for many' (Mark 10:45).

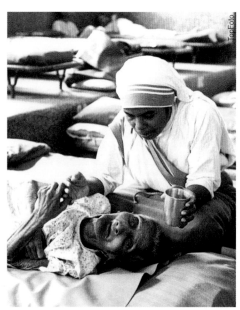

Jesus believed in putting others first

Test yourself

1 Fill in each of the gaps below.
  The Ten ....
  .... God only
  Do not .... God's name
  Keep the Lord's day ....
  Do not ....
  Do not ....
  Do not .... your ....
  Do not .... your ....

  Honour your ....
  Do not commit ....
  Do not commit ....

  Jesus' summary of the Ten ....
  Love .... with all your ....
  Love your .... as ....

2 Match up correctly the two parts of each Beatitude.

Happy are the humble		They shall receive mercy
Happy are those who mourn		They shall be called children of God
Happy are the meek		Theirs is the kingdom of heaven
Happy are those who hunger for righteousness		They shall be comforted
Happy are the merciful		They shall inherit the earth
Happy are the pure in heart		They shall be satisfied
Happy are the peacemakers		Theirs is the kingdom of heaven
Happy are those who are persecuted for righteousness		They shall see God

Examination question

a **Explain briefly how Christians might reflect the teachings of the Beatitudes in their everyday lives.**   *(2 marks)*

b **'The Ten Commandments are out of date in today's world.'
   Do you agree? Give reasons for your answer, showing that you have thought about more than one point of view.**   *(6 marks)*

Exam tip

To gain more than 4 marks in a 6-mark evaluation question, you have to argue from more than one viewpoint.

Christian marriage

The rite of marriage

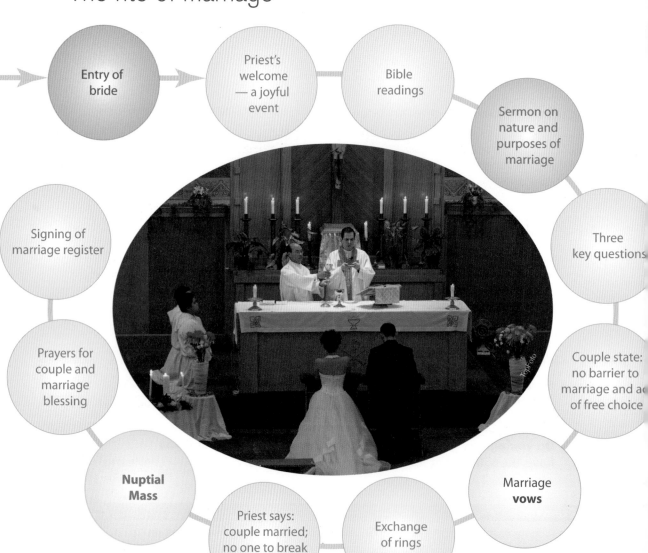

- Entry of bride
- Priest's welcome — a joyful event
- Bible readings
- Sermon on nature and purposes of marriage
- Three key questions
- Couple state: no barrier to marriage and act of free choice
- Marriage **vows**
- Exchange of rings
- Priest says: couple married; no one to break the bond
- **Nuptial Mass**
- Prayers for couple and marriage blessing
- Signing of marriage register

What is marriage?

Marriage is a **sacramental covenant**, i.e. a sacred bond between the couple, made by God with the couple. The ring is a visible sign of this and other signs in the ceremony are:

- It takes place in a church.
- The couple make solemn vows.
- There is a Nuptial Mass.

The three key questions

- Will the couple give themselves freely and unreservedly to one another?
- Will they love and honour one another until death separates them?
- Will they accept children lovingly as a gift from God, giving them a Christian upbringing?

The vows

The couple promise to love and care for one another for the rest of their lives.

The nature of marriage
Mixed marriages

Marriages between people of different denominations or different faiths are allowed, but need the permission of the diocesan authorities. There is always a time of preparation with the priest before the marriage and, in the case of mixed marriages, this preparation will be even more necessary.

A sign of lifelong love and faithfulness — marriage is **permanent** and **exclusive**

Sex within marriage

Sexual intercourse expresses most intimately the couple's love for one another. It sets a seal on the marriage. It is meant to be **unitive** (an act in which the two become physically as well as spiritually one) and **procreative** (open to the possibility of conceiving a child). Use of contraception is therefore a sin.

Roman Catholic views on sexuality

- It is a gift from God, to be enjoyed responsibly (within marriage).

- All forms of sex outside marriage are sinful. **Pre-marital sex** trivialises what is a sacred gift, and **adultery** is an act of betrayal and breaks the sixth commandment.

- **Chastity** is a virtue that all unmarried Roman Catholics should practise.

- Some are called to **celibacy** as a way of showing their total devotion to God.

Other Christian views on sexuality

Protestant churches also teach that sexual relationships belong within marriage, and are particularly opposed to adultery. But some Christians argue that times have changed and that sexual relationships between two people who are in a loving relationship, though not married, are not sinful. They are, however, opposed to **casual sex**, which devalues God's gift.

The Silver Ring Thing

This is a movement that began in the USA and has spread to Europe. Boys and girls make a promise of sexual purity until they marry. As a sign of that promise, they wear a silver ring.

Responsible parenthood

This means being prepared to accept with love any children as a gift from God, but natural family planning is an acceptable way of spacing them out. It also means giving children love and security. Parents should provide a Christian upbringing by the example they set in the home, regular prayer, etc. and by encouraging them to attend church and to receive all the sacraments that are open to them.

Adoption and fostering

Responsible care of children is a key duty of the Roman Catholic Church. Giving vulnerable children love and protection is a reflection of the example set by Jesus.

This silver ring is worn by teenagers as a sign of their promise to remain sexually pure

Christians see children as a gift from God

> Tell these women to take their children away, Jesus. You're too important and too busy to be bothered with a bunch of kids.

> Leave them alone. God's kingdom belongs to them. You will have to become like children if you want to enter it. Let them come to me so that I can give them a blessing.

There are many Roman Catholic **adoption** and **fostering** agencies. Adoption means that couples become the legal parents of children whose birth parents cannot or choose not to look after them. Fostering may be permanent or temporary, long term or short term. Responsibility for children is shared with the social services.

Why marriages fail

Support for failing marriages
- Roman Catholic support agencies, e.g. Marriage Care, Accord
- marriage counsellors
- advice from the parish priest
- reading the Bible
- prayer
- receiving the sacraments, particularly the **Eucharist** and **Reconciliation**
- family and friends

Divorce, remarriage and annulment
The law

	Unreasonable behaviour	
Infidelity	Irretrievable breakdown of marriage	Desertion
2 years' separation — both partners agree		5 years' separation

Jesus' teaching on divorce and remarriage

Jesus taught that marriage was intended by God to be lifelong, and that the law permitting divorce was a concession to human weakness. In marriage the two became one. They were united by God, and humans should not interfere with this.

Jesus' teaching about remarriage is recorded in two Gospels. According to Mark, Jesus said that remarriage after divorce was tantamount to adultery. According to Matthew, however, Jesus accepted remarriage after divorce if one partner had been unfaithful.

Roman Catholic teaching on divorce and remarriage

The Church believes that Jesus was laying down a rule for his followers to obey, and that vows made in the name of God cannot be dissolved. Divorce is a 'grave offence' (Catechism of the Catholic Church) though the Church gives support to divorced people.

Remarriage after divorce makes matters even worse, and those who remarry after divorce may not receive the Eucharist. They are, however, encouraged to attend Mass, as in other ways they often keep the faith and want to bring up their children as Christians.

Roman Catholic teaching on annulment

On rare occasions, the Church may grant an annulment, for example, if it can be shown that one of the partners was forced into the marriage, suffered from mental problems at the time, never intended to keep the vows or was not baptised at the time of the marriage. An annulment is a declaration that a true marriage never took place. This means that the partners are free to 'remarry'.

Protestant teaching on divorce and remarriage

Attitudes vary in the Church of England. Some priests take the Roman Catholic view. Others will not allow remarriage in church on the grounds that the vows cannot be made twice, but they offer a service of Marriage Blessing after a civil marriage ceremony. Yet other priests adopt the attitude of the other Protestant churches. They believe that marriage is intended to be lifelong, but that people are human and make mistakes. They think Jesus' teaching was an ideal rather than a law, and they point out that he was always willing to give people a second chance and a fresh start. So they will allow the remarriage in church of people who have been divorced.

TopFoto

Prince Charles and Camilla Parker Bowles had a civil ceremony followed by a marriage blessing in St George's Chapel, Windsor

Jenny and Dave

- Aged 28 and 32
- Married for 2 years
- Two children
- Jenny — Anglican
- Dave — Roman Catholic

Key words

adoption	divorce	pre-marital sex
adultery	Eucharist	procreative
annulment	exclusive	Reconciliation
casual sex	fostering	sacramental covenant
celibacy	Nuptial Mass	unitive
chastity	permanent	vows

Test yourself

1 True or false?

	TRUE	FALSE
Mass at a wedding is known as a Nuptial Mass.		
Mixed marriages are not allowed in the Roman Catholic Church.		
All Christians should practise celibacy.		
Adultery is forbidden in the Ten Commandments.		

Chastity is a virtue.

The American sexual purity movement is called the Golden Ring Thing.

Jesus believed that marriage is intended to be for life.

Remarriage after divorce is never allowed by the Roman Catholic Church.

Remarriage after divorce is never allowed by the Church of England.

An annulment is a statement that a true marriage never took place.

2 Fill in the chart with six reasons why marriages sometimes break down.

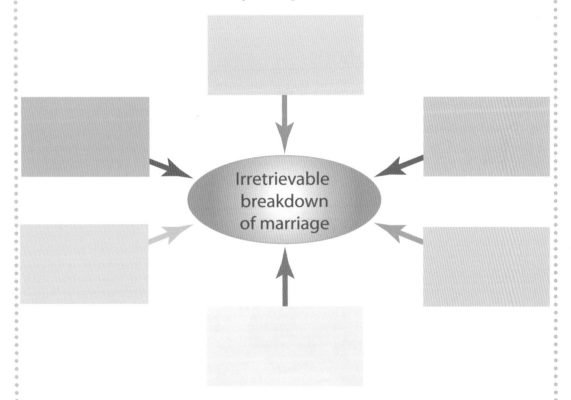

Irretrievable breakdown of marriage

Examination question

a Describe what happens at a Roman Catholic wedding ceremony. *(6 marks)*

b 'Remarriage in church after a divorce should never be allowed.' What do you think? Explain your opinion. *(3 marks)*

Exam tip

Before answering a question, always think about the command (trigger) word. This is the word, usually at the start of a question, that tells you what you have to do. If it says 'describe', you do not need to give any explanation. You would not lose marks for doing so, but you would not gain any, so you would penalise yourself by losing valuable time.

Christian vocation

All baptised Christians have the **vocation** to live holy lives and serve God.

Holy Orders (ordination)

Some men receive a special vocation to the **sacred ministry**. The three orders of ministry are: bishops, priests and deacons.

The rite of ordination of priests

This ceremony goes back to the 12 apostles. Its central features are the **laying on of hands** and invoking the **Holy Spirit**. The priest receives the power of the Holy Spirit to fulfil his calling.

They promise to serve the Church, study and pray, celebrate the **sacraments** and obey the bishop

The priests are called forward by name and asked if they are willing to serve the Church

Their prostration is a sign of submission to and dependence on God

The Peace is shared and the priest celebrates the Eucharist with the bishop and his fellow priests

The bishop lays his hands on each man's head, praying for the gift of the Holy Spirit

The priest is **anointed** on the hands as a symbol of his choice by God and his readiness to do God's work. He is given a chalice, paten and vestments for celebrating the Eucharist

The role and work of the priest

Priests are co-workers with the bishop, and they act as **mediators** between Christ and his Church, especially when they celebrate the Eucharist. They represent Jesus to the believing community. They have many sacramental and **pastoral** duties:

- administering sacraments
- leading prayer and worship
- proclaiming the gospel and teaching the faith
- looking after the people in the bishop's parish
- being a servant to Christ and his Church, i.e. putting the needs of others first

The role of deacons

Most deacons go on to become priests, but some remain deacons all their lives, and they may be married. The deacon's role is that of a servant, reflecting Jesus' example:

- assisting bishops and priests with the sacraments, especially the Eucharist
- assisting at and blessing marriages
- proclaiming the gospel and preaching
- taking funerals
- being involved in social and charitable works

Ordination of women to the priesthood

According to Roman Catholic law, only men can be ordained. Many Protestant churches have long had female ministers and in 1994 the first women priests were ordained in the Church of England, though many Anglicans still disagree with this.

Arguments against women priests	Arguments for women priests
Jesus chose men to be his disciples, and male priesthood is a part of Church tradition and law. In the Early Church women were made priests, but this was done by heretical churches and linked to their false beliefs.	In the first century, choosing women as disciples would have been a non-starter but, had he lived now, Jesus would have included women as he regarded them highly.
Some of Paul's teaching in his letters stated that women should not lead worship.	In other parts of Paul's letters he accepted women as having authority, and he also wrote that, for those who are baptised, gender distinctions have no meaning. In any case, society has now changed.
Such major decisions should be agreed on by all the churches before implementing them. The ordination of women in the Anglican Church has led to disunity within it and damaged ecumenical relationships.	Sometimes a stand has to be made or nothing would ever change.
Men and women are essentially different. Women have important but different roles to play.	Women have a unique contribution to make to the priesthood because they are different from men.

Celibacy of the priesthood

Celibacy of the priesthood has been a part of Roman Catholic canon law for many centuries, though at least some of Jesus' disciples were married and so were priests in the Early Church. Celibacy is a positive act of giving oneself to God rather than a negative act of 'doing without'.

Arguments for celibate priests	Arguments for married priests
Jesus was unmarried and celibacy has long been part of canon law.	Jesus chose disciples who were married and it was not an issue in the Early Church.
It shows the priest's total commitment to Christ and his Church. Marriage would interfere with that and distract him from his duties.	More people would respond to the call to the priesthood and being married would be enriching. Married priests could give better advice and support to families.
There could be times when priestly and family duties were in conflict.	Many married people have very demanding jobs but manage both. It would be no worse for a priest.

Religious vocation

Fotolia

Some men and women are called to become monks and nuns in either contemplative or apostolic orders. After some years as novices, they make three vows:

- poverty — they own no personal possessions
- chastity — absolute sexual purity
- obedience — to the rules of the order and to the abbot

Contemplative orders

Contemplative orders are enclosed. There is total devotion to worship, private prayer and study.

Apostolic orders

Again there is devotion to regular worship, prayer and study, but members of **apostolic orders** also serve the community, for example, working with homeless people, teaching in schools.

Lay ministry

Lay people (the **laity**) refers to people who are not ordained or members of monastic communities. They have a key role to play in the life of the Church and the world by serving God faithfully in their everyday lives.

Use whatever talents God has blessed them with to the best of their ability, to the glory of God and in the service of others

Develop spiritually through prayer, receiving the sacraments, Bible study, going on pilgrimages and retreats

How members of the laity fulfil their Christian vocation

Being loving husbands/wives/ parents/children and being reliable employers/ employees/students

Practical service of others, e.g. giving regularly to charities, joining the Society of Saint Vincent de Paul (SVP)

The parable of the talents: Matthew 25:14–30

Jesus' parable (a story with a meaning) teaches people to make good use of the gifts they have been given by God. In the story, three servants were given differing sums of money by their master. They were expected to use the money to make a profit for him. Two of the servants doubled what they had been given and were rewarded. The third, too lazy to be bothered, simply buried it in a safe place and then gave it back when his master sent for him. He made the feeble excuse that he was afraid to risk losing it in any business venture because he would be punished. His master saw through his excuse and said he should at least have gained interest on it by investing it. The servant was thrown out and the money he had been given was given to the servant who had made the most.

Case study

Pete

- Aged 15
- Attends St Thomas More school
- Interests: football, swimming, films
- Wants to work in a sports centre
- Roman Catholic

I enjoy going out with my friends on a weekend and I play football whenever I can. I realise how lucky I am — I've everything going for me. So I've got involved with Youth SVP at my school. Once a week I go to the local sports centre and help at a swimming session for severely disabled teenagers. I get as much out of it as they do, and it's my way of showing God how grateful I am for the great life I have. When I leave school, I'll join my parish SVP.

Key words

anointed	laying on of hands	sacraments
apostolic orders	mediators	sacred ministry
contemplative orders	ordination	vocation
Holy Spirit	parables	
laity	pastoral	

Test yourself

1 List three duties of a priest.

2 What vows do monks and nuns make?

3 What is the difference between contemplative and apostolic orders of monks and nuns?

4 What are 'lay people'?

Examination question

a Explain the meaning of the term 'vocation'. *(2 marks)*

> The vicar at my church is a woman. I think you have to move with the times and anyway, she's a great asset to the community.

> In my church we don't have women as priests. We think it's better for the parish community to have a man and also that we are following Jesus' practice.

Exam tip

The command (trigger) word 'explain' requires you to show both knowledge and understanding. You need to develop the points you made, rather than give a simple list of points.

b Explain why some Christians support and others oppose the ordination of women to the priesthood. *(6 marks)*

Christian reconciliation

The Sacrament of Reconciliation

Sin and forgiveness

Sin is an offence against God that often hurts others also. Mortal sins are more serious than venial sins as they alienate the person from God. Christians believe that God is merciful and that Jesus died to break down the barrier of sin that cuts humans off from God. This means that if people turn to God in **penitence** and ask to make a fresh start, God will always forgive. **Forgiveness** is about wiping the slate clean and restoring the relationship. Because mortal sins are so serious, however, they can be forgiven only through the **Sacrament of Reconciliation**.

The Rite of Reconciliation

After his resurrection, Jesus gave his apostles the authority to forgive sins. Roman Catholics believe that this authority has been passed down through the priesthood, and that Roman Catholic priests are able in this sacrament to declare God's forgiveness of sins and to reconcile with the Church those who are penitent. It is often used as a preparation for receiving other sacraments and also to enable a dying person to die in a state of grace.

The parable of the forgiving father: Luke 15:11–32

The point of this story is that God is always willing to let someone make a fresh start. There are no limits to his forgiveness.

The younger of two sons asked his father for his share of the inheritance. He then went abroad and blew it all on wild living. So when famine hit the country, he had to find work. He looked after pigs, but was still so hungry that he could have eaten their food. He decided to go home, ask to be forgiven and to be taken on as a servant.

His father had been looking out for him all this time. When he saw his son, he ran to greet him. He cut short the boy's apology, sending for a ring, shoes and the best clothes for his son to wear, and ordering the specially fattened calf to be killed and cooked for a celebration meal.

When the older son learned what was going on, he was furious and refused to join the party. His father went to him and begged him. He told his older son that he loved him and that everything would one day be his; but at the same time, he could not help rejoicing when his son who had been as good as dead to him returned.

Stages in the Rite of Reconciliation

The penitent spends time alone in prayer and meditation

The penitent goes to a priest

The priest declares God's forgiveness, using a special prayer

'May God give you pardon and peace, and I absolve you from your sins, in the name of the Father, and of the Son, and of the Holy Spirit.'

The penitent confesses his/her sins, expressing sorrow and a wish to be forgiven

The priest sets a **penance**, to help the person get back on the right path

The priest gives helpful advice

 Case study

Roisin

- Aged 20 years
- University student
- Intended career: journalism
- Interests: watching Gaelic football, socialising
- Roman Catholic

Key words

forgiveness
penance
penitence
Sacrament of Reconciliation
sin

I guess I'm just like most people. I'm not perfect, but I like to help people when I can, and I try not to hurt people. I commit lots of what I would call small sins, so I don't have to go to confession. But for the last few years I have always gone in Holy Week. My priest always gives good advice on how to lead a better life, and the Sacrament of Reconciliation somehow enriches the celebration of Easter.

Test yourself

1 The rite of the Sacrament of Reconciliation is summarised below in a number of sentences. Put them in the right order:

.... The penitent confesses his/her sins, expressing sorrow and a wish to be forgiven

.... The penitent goes to a priest

.... The priest declares God's forgiveness, using a special prayer

.... The priest gives helpful advice

.... The penitent spends time alone in prayer and meditation

.... 'May God give you pardon and peace, and I absolve you from your sins, in the name of the Father, and of the Son, and of the Holy Spirit.'

.... The priest sets a penance, to help the person get back on the right path

2 Explain the meaning of each of the following terms:

Sin..

....

Mortal sin...

....

Venial sin..

....

3 Explain how the parable of the forgiving father gets across the point that there are no limits to God's forgiveness.

....

....

....

....

....

Examination question

'There is no point in the Sacrament of Reconciliation.'

What do you think? Explain your opinion.

(3 marks)

Exam tip

3-mark evaluation questions do not require you to give two points of view. They want you to say what you think about the issue, giving reasons for the opinion you hold. You need to make sure that you read the stem (the quotation at the start of the question) very carefully so that your answer is focused and relevant.

Crime and punishment

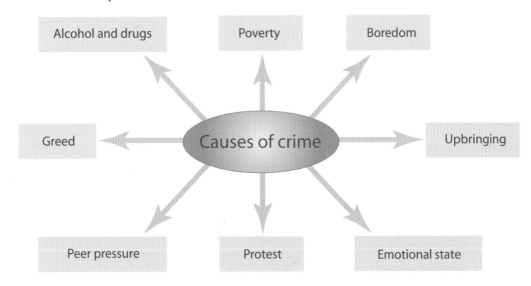

Alcohol and drugs

Poverty

Boredom

Greed

Causes of crime

Upbringing

Peer pressure

Protest

Emotional state

Forms of punishment

There are many different types of punishment that a judge or magistrate can give an offender. When deciding on a sentence, the offender's past history is taken into account, along with any mitigating circumstances and the seriousness of the offence.

Imprisonment

There are four categories of adult **prison**, ranging from high security for offenders who might pose a threat to society (category A) to open prisons for those nearing the end of a sentence or who are not dangerous

- The conditions in many prisons are very bad:
  - overcrowding and poor sanitation
  - lack of opportunity for education and work training
  - bullying
  - being locked up for almost the whole day
- Young people who need to be kept in custody may be put in:
  - young offender institutions
  - secure training centres
  - local authority secure children's homes
- Adult prisoners who have behaved well in prison, who show signs of remorse and who are unlikely to pose a threat to society, may be given parole, which involves early release with monitoring by a parole officer and sometimes electronic tagging.

TopFoto

Imprisonment is just one type of punishment that can be given to offenders

Probation

Offenders are under the supervision of a **probation** officer for a set period of time. They meet up regularly to discuss progress.

Community service

Offenders have to carry out unpaid work that benefits the community, in their own time for a set period of hours.

Fines

These are sums of money paid to the court and are used for a variety of offences.

Electronic tagging and curfews

These are intended to enable the police to monitor the whereabouts of offenders and restrict their movements.

ASBOs

These prevent individuals from being in an area where they have caused problems for the community in the past.

Aims of punishment

Magistrates and judges give sentences that are intended to achieve particular aims. You need to know about four aims of punishment (though there are more). Increasingly the authorities are interested in restorative justice,

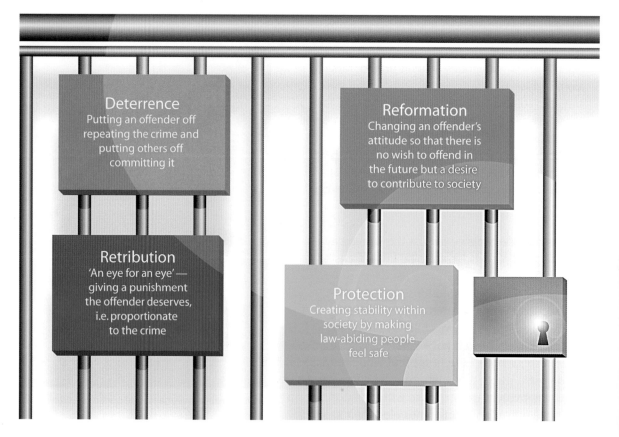

Deterrence
Putting an offender off repeating the crime and putting others off committing it

Reformation
Changing an offender's attitude so that there is no wish to offend in the future but a desire to contribute to society

Retribution
'An eye for an eye' — giving a punishment the offender deserves, i.e. proportionate to the crime

Protection
Creating stability within society by making law-abiding people feel safe

Christian attitudes to crime and punishment

Christians believe that the law gives stability to society and should always be obeyed, unless it conflicts with God's will as revealed in the Bible, the teachings of the Church and conscience. Jesus said: 'Give to Caesar what belongs to him and to God what belongs to him.' So Christians accept that punishment may be needed to ensure that justice is carried out and to enable offenders to recognise the hurt they have caused and come to terms with it. But punishment should always go hand in hand with forgiveness; offenders should always have the chance to make a fresh start and victims should be helped to move on and not be consumed by bitterness and the desire for revenge. So for most Christians, reformation is the most important aim of punishment.

A recently released prisoner trying on clothes donated by a church

The Church also gives practical help to offenders who want to make a fresh start. Prisons have chaplains to celebrate Mass and other sacraments and to give support. The SVP helps offenders and their families, and some Christian employers are willing to give ex-offenders a job.

Reformation

Restorative justice: offenders make amends to their victims (e.g. repairing damage) or meet their victims to talk things through

Prisoners working in an upholstery workshop at HM Prison Manchester

Education: offenders learn literacy skills, take exams, train in vocational skills

Gives offenders a second chance and victims and society a chance to forgive and move on

Those in prison contribute positively to society instead of feeling cut off from it

Jesus said: 'Love your enemies and pray for those who persecute you'

'Forgive us our sins, as we forgive those who have sinned against us'

Example: learning Braille and transcribing books for blind people

Example: the Dartmoor Storybook Dads project helps fathers and their children

Christian views about the death penalty (capital punishment)

Many countries still carry the death penalty out for serious offences, e.g. the USA, but in the UK it was abolished 50 years ago. Some Christians would like it to be restored, putting forward a number of arguments for it.

The Catechism of the Catholic Church allows for the **death penalty** in very serious cases, where it seems the only appropriate response to a terrible crime, but at the same time states its preference for 'bloodless solutions', and Pope John Paul II was opposed to it.

Many other denominations, e.g. Anglican and Quaker, have made official statements opposing it, and most Christians take this position.

For the death penalty	Against the death penalty
Justice — 'an eye for an eye' — a murderer forfeits his or her own life	The 'eye for an eye' mentality encourages revenge, which is a negative and harmful attitude. Jesus asked God to forgive those who had nailed him to the cross
It shows love for the victims of serious crime	It does not show love for one's neighbour or for enemies
A second chance is not deserved — the victim doesn't have one	The offender has no chance to reform, to make a fresh start and become a useful citizen
The woman referred to in the column opposite had committed adultery, not murder. Maybe Jesus' verdict on a murderer would have been different	When Jesus was asked to pass sentence on a woman caught in the act of adultery (a capital offence in first-century Israel), he said those without sin should cast the first stone. He told her that he did not condemn her; she should go but not repeat her sin. He gave her a second chance
It provides absolute protection for society	Many murderers are not a danger to society as a whole and, if they are released, it is release on licence
It is the most effective deterrent	Evidence from the USA shows that it does not work as a deterrent
Forensic science makes wrongful execution more unlikely	Innocent people have been executed
The families of the victim never recover from their trauma — and they are innocent, too	It causes deep emotional and psychological trauma to the families of those executed — and the families are innocent

Case study

Sister Helen Prejean, CSV

- Born in Louisiana in 1939 and became a nun in 1957
- Became involved in prison work in 1981
- Became the pen pal of a man on death row in Louisiana
- Visited him, became his spiritual advisor and was with him as he went to the electric chair
- Seeing what life was like on death row and witnessing his death led to her becoming a prominent campaigner against the death penalty
- She also founded Survive, an organisation that provides counselling for the families of victims of violence
- She sees two rights as absolutely fundamental: the right not to be tortured and the right not to be killed
- She believes in the teaching of Jesus not to reply to hate with hate

Sister Helen Prejean

The parable of the unmerciful servant: Matthew 18:23–35

Peter had asked Jesus how often he should forgive someone who kept on sinning against him: was seven times enough? Jesus replied: 'Not seven times but seventy times seven', i.e. always be prepared to forgive. To illustrate this, and also the importance of being prepared to forgive others if people wished to be forgiven by God, he told the following story.

A king was settling his accounts and realised that one of his servants owed him a huge amount of money. So he sent for him, demanding repayment and threatening enslavement otherwise for the man and his family. The servant desperately begged for more time and the king felt so sorry for him that he just cancelled the debt. On his way back to his duties, the servant came across a man who owed him a small amount of money. He grabbed him by the throat, demanding immediate repayment. He was not prepared to grant the man's request for more time, but had him thrown into prison. The king was furious when he heard what had happened. He told the servant he should have shown the same forgiveness that he had been shown. He then had the servant imprisoned.

Key words

ASBO
community service
death penalty
deterrence
electronic tagging
fines
justice
prison
probation
protection
reformation
restorative justice
retribution

Test yourself

1 Explain briefly why people might commit crimes.

2 Name one country that still carries out the death penalty.

3 Name one country that does not carry out the death penalty.

4 In the table below match up correctly each aim of punishment with its explanation.

Deterrence		To change the attitude of the offender
Protection		To put the offender off committing crime again
Reformation		To give the offender what he/she deserves
Retribution		To keep society safe

Examination question

 BREAKING NEWS! 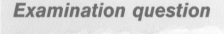 Inspector of prisons slams three prisons over appalling conditions for prisoners!

1 **Outline the concerns that many people have about some prisons in the UK.** *(4 marks)*

2 **'Convicted murderers should always receive the death penalty.' Do you agree? Give reasons for your answer, showing that you have thought about more than one point of view. Refer to Christian teachings in your answer.** *(6 marks)*

Exam tip

The command word 'outline' requires only a brief summary of the key points; a detailed description is not required.

Prejudice and discrimination

Prejudice

Prejudice refers to what goes on in the mind. It consists of pre-judging, i.e. holding fixed views on someone or something without good reason. Prejudiced views are irrational, for example, thinking that all women are bad car drivers.

Discrimination

Discrimination is putting prejudice into action. It is treating someone in a particular way (usually negatively) without good reason, for example, refusing to employ someone as a taxi driver because she is a woman.

Causes of prejudice and discrimination

There are many reasons but the fundamental cause is ignorance. Lack of knowledge and understanding underlies most prejudice.

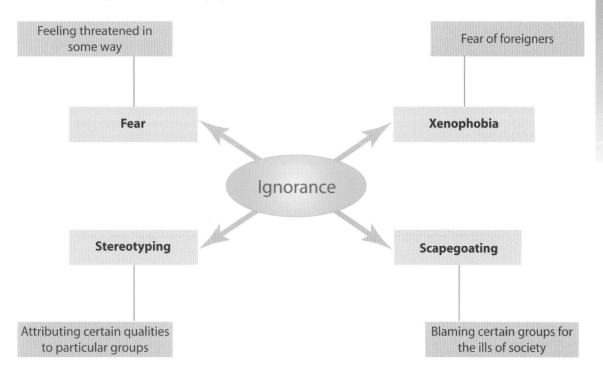

Feeling threatened in some way

Fear of foreigners

Fear

Xenophobia

Ignorance

Stereotyping

Scapegoating

Attributing certain qualities to particular groups

Blaming certain groups for the ills of society

Types of prejudice and discrimination

You have to know about four types:

- colour and racial — particularly towards black people
- religious — often towards Muslims
- gender — usually towards women
- disability — towards both mentally and physically disabled people

All these forms of discrimination are illegal. The law covers many areas, including employment, education, benefits and housing. It also deals with verbal discrimination, e.g. the kind of speech that might encourage racial

TopFoto

The success of Dame Tanni Grey-Thompson has helped raise the profile of athletes with disabilities

hatred, or verbal harassment of female employees by employers. Victims of discrimination can take their case to tribunal. But discrimination continues to be a major problem in the UK because the law cannot dictate how people think. It cannot prosecute prejudice, and prejudice quickly spills over into action. The law may also not be able to give protection if:

- the discrimination is very subtle
- there are no witnesses
- witnesses are afraid to give evidence
- the victim does not report anything for fear of what will follow
- the victim is not as articulate or well represented legally as the discriminator

Christian views on prejudice and discrimination

All Christians agree that prejudice and discrimination are sinful. The Bible makes it clear that all people are children of God, to be treated with the respect and dignity that their status as human beings deserves. In the past, Christians have been guilty of all four types of discrimination, but the Church has long recognised that this is incompatible with the teaching of the New Testament in particular. Christians believe in equality: that all human beings have equal value and should be treated the same. They also believe in justice: that all human beings have the same right to fair and equal treatment.

All one in Christ: Galatians 3:28

In his letter to the Christians of Galatia, Paul stated that racial, gender and social distinctions had no meaning for God, and that it should be the same for Christians also.

The parable of the Good Samaritan: Luke 10:25–37

When Jesus told a scribe that the way to gain eternal life was to love God and one's neighbour, the scribe asked: 'And who is my neighbour?' Jesus replied with the following story in which a man was ignored by his fellow countrymen and helped by an enemy. Jesus was making the point that being a neighbour has nothing to do with culture, religious belief or race.

A Jew was mugged as he was on his way to Jericho. A priest and Levite (religious leaders who worked in the Temple) came by but crossed over the road to avoid him. It was a Samaritan who stopped to help, despite the centuries of enmity between Jews and Samaritans. He bandaged the man's wounds and took him on his donkey to an inn, where he paid for his keep, offering to pay any more that was needed when he returned.

When asked who had been the neighbour, the scribe said: 'The one who showed pity.' 'Go and do the same,' Jesus replied.

Key words

discrimination
prejudice
scapegoating
stereotyping
xenophobia

By word: in sermons and speeches, by refusing to join in racist conversation

By example: parents and other adults setting a good example

How can Christians counter prejudice and discrimination?

By action: protest marches, writing to MPs, befriending vulnerable groups

Case study

Martin Luther King

- Born in the USA in 1929 — a black American
- Became a Baptist minister and the leader of the black community in his town
- Led the bus boycott in 1955 after Rosa Parkes was arrested for refusing to give up her seat on the bus to a white man, and this resulted in desegregation of buses
- Became leader of the civil rights movement — involved in a wide variety of non-violent protests that led gradually to desegregation of schools, restaurants etc.
- Despite threats to his life and a bomb left outside his house, he constantly advocated non-violence — the only way to neutralise evil was by responding to it with love
- Gave the 'I have a dream speech' at a huge rally in Washington, speaking of his dream that one day all races, religions etc. would live together in harmony
- Awarded the Nobel Peace Prize in 1964
- Black people given the vote in 1965
- Assassinated in 1968

TopFoto

Test yourself

1 Name two causes of prejudice.

2 Name two forms of discrimination.

3 Fill in the gaps in the following:

Jesus told a .... about a .... man who was travelling
to.............................. He was .... and left for dead. First of all a ....
came by, but he totally .... the injured man. Then came a ....
and he did the same. Eventually a .... came along. It was surprising that he
stopped to help, as .... and .... were bitter enemies. Anyway, the
.... bandaged the man up, put him on his .... and took him to an
.... where he .... the innkeeper to look after the injured man.
He promised to pay any .... that he owed on his return.

Examination question

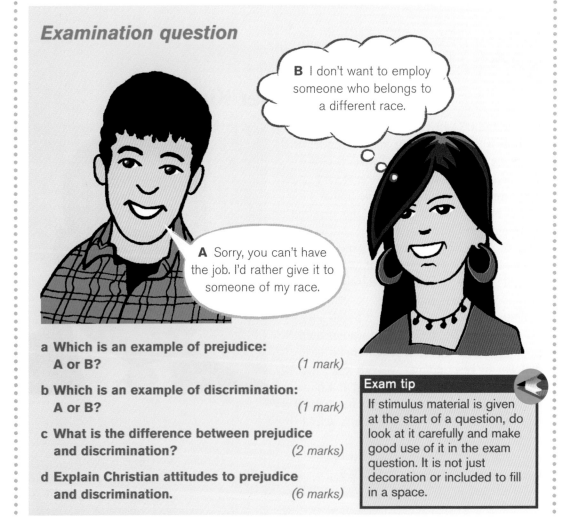

B I don't want to employ someone who belongs to a different race.

A Sorry, you can't have the job. I'd rather give it to someone of my race.

a Which is an example of prejudice: A or B? *(1 mark)*

b Which is an example of discrimination: A or B? *(1 mark)*

c What is the difference between prejudice and discrimination? *(2 marks)*

d Explain Christian attitudes to prejudice and discrimination. *(6 marks)*

Exam tip

If stimulus material is given at the start of a question, do look at it carefully and make good use of it in the exam question. It is not just decoration or included to fill in a space.

Christian healing

The Sacrament of the Anointing of the Sick

Healing was a prominent part of Jesus' ministry, and the apostles also exercised this gift. The healing was both physical and spiritual. The Church also developed a ministry to the dying.

The ministry of healing through the laying on of hands and anointing with oil was practised from the earliest days of the Church. The **Sacrament of the Anointing of the Sick** may be given to anyone who is seriously ill or who is facing major surgery.

Holy Communion given: if the person is dying, it is known as **Viaticum**, spiritual food for the journey ahead

Prayer is offered: specific to the sick person's needs

Sprinkling with holy water: reminder of the grace given at baptism

The Sacrament of the Anointing of the Sick

The laying on of hands: a symbol of the Holy Spirit's strengthening power

Anointing of the forehead and hands with holy oil with a special prayer: symbol of healing and giving inner strength to those about to die

Effects of the Sacrament of the Anointing of the Sick

- healing in some cases
- peace of mind and ability to come to terms with continued illness
- spiritual growth and acceptance of illness as sharing in Jesus' suffering
- sense of God's closeness even in darkest hours
- those about to die can face death calmly with awareness of sins forgiven and God's love
- spiritual strengthening and comfort for friends and relatives

Case study

Chris

- Aged 16
- Attends St David's High
- Interests: computer games, films
- Roman Catholic

I'm not really into God or religion, but when my gran was dying, I was there with my parents when Fr Jones gave her the Sacrament of the Anointing of the Sick. I didn't really understand the meaning of everything he did, but it made a big difference to gran. She became very peaceful and she wasn't afraid of death. In fact, it helped us all cope better.

Dying and the afterlife

Christians believe that death is a part of life and not to be feared, as it is not the end. Thanks to Jesus' death and **resurrection**, eternal life with God is available to all believers. The body perishes, but the soul lives on, to be clothed with a new 'spiritual body' appropriate to the new form of life. These beliefs are reflected in the Roman Catholic funeral rites and in the practice of praying for the dead.

Roman Catholic funeral rites

TopFoto

Burial or cremation

↑

Coffin sprinkled with holy water

↑

Prayers, committing dead person to God's care

↑

Requiem Mass

↑

White sheet on coffin (symbol of baptismal robe) or cross or Gospel book

Coffin taken into church the night before or **vigil** (wake) at home

↓

Priest greets mourners at church door

↓

Coffin sprinkled with holy water: sign of dying and rising with Christ at baptism →

Roman Catholic beliefs about life after death

- Death is not the end.
- Resurrection of the body was taught by Jesus, the New Testament generally and is in Christian **creeds.**
- Two types of judgement:
  – 'particular judgement' of each individual immediately after death
  – 'general judgement' of all humanity on Judgement Day
- Those who die in mortal sin and are totally unrepentant are cut off from God (hell).
- The very devout and virtuous go immediately into God's presence (heaven).
- Most need purification before being with God.
- **Purgatory** is a state of purification and spiritual cleansing that enables further spiritual growth before being admitted to God's presence.
- Those in purgatory may be helped by Masses and prayers offered on their behalf or by works of charity done in their name.

Key words
creeds
purgatory
Requiem Mass
resurrection
Sacrament of the Anointing of the Sick
Viaticum
vigil

Test yourself

1 The laying on of hands and anointing with holy oil are the key parts of the Sacrament of the Anointing of the Sick. What do they symbolise?

....

....

2 Explain the symbolism of sprinkling with holy water. ....

....

3 What is Viaticum? ....

4 To whom is it given? ....

5 Explain the two types of judgement that each human faces, according to Roman Catholic teaching.

....

....

6 What is purgatory? ....

....

7 Why do Roman Catholics think it is important to pray for the dead and to hold Requiem Masses?

....

....

....

....

....

Examination question

a Describe Roman Catholic funeral rites.

b 'There is no point in giving the Sacrament of the Anointing of the Sick to someone who is about to die.' *(6 marks)*

Do you agree? Give reasons for your answer, showing that you have thought about more than one point of view.

(6 marks)

Exam tip

Try to use technical terms, e.g. purgatory, Viaticum. But make sure that you understand and use them correctly.

Respect for human life — at its start

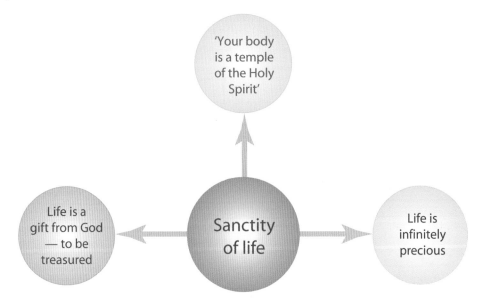

'Your body is a temple of the Holy Spirit'

Life is a gift from God — to be treasured

Sanctity of life

Life is infinitely precious

Contraception

This refers to artificial ways of preventing a woman from becoming pregnant.

Roman Catholic teaching

- Contraception is sinful.

- The main purpose of sexual intercourse is procreative.

- **Contraception** either prevents pregnancy or acts as an abortifacient, which is tantamount to murder.

- Natural methods of family planning, e.g. tracking the rhythm of the menstrual cycle, are permitted as these do not set out to interfere with God's plan.

Protestant teaching

- Contraception is acceptable.

- God gave humans the capacity for responsible decision-making and this includes decisions about having children.

- Procreation is not the primary purpose of sexual intercourse.

- There may be good reasons for not wanting children: poverty, wanting to space the births, a genetic disorder or the HIV virus carried by one partner.

- If unmarried people are determined to have sexual relationships, then using contraception is the responsible action to take.

Abortion
UK law

Selective reduction of foetuses in multiple pregnancy

Risk to physical health of woman

Risk to physical health of existing children

Risk to mental health of woman

Up to 24 weeks

Risk to mental health of existing children

Legal grounds for abortion

Probability of grave permanent injury to woman's physical health

Up to term

Substantial risk of severe physical disability in foetus

Probability of grave permanent injury to woman's mental health

Risk to life of woman

Substantial risk of severe mental disability in foetus

Pro-choice

Maternal rights come first.

The mother is more fully alive than a foetus.

She should decide what happens in and to her body.

Pro-life

Foetal rights come first.

The foetus is fully alive as a human being with potential.

The foetus is vulnerable and needs protection.

Neil Bromhall/SPL

A 5-month-old foetus

When does life begin?

Biological life begins with the fertilisation of the egg by the sperm, but what is meant here is at what stage is it meaningful life, i.e. life with rights? There are different views on this:

- At conception
  - the **pro-life** view taken by the Roman Catholic Church and many Protestants
  - from the moment of fertilisation, a new person with potential, a human being complete with a soul, has come into existence
- At birth
  - the **pro-choice** view
  - independent life only starts at birth; until that point the foetus is totally dependent on the mother
- **Viability**
  - the view taken by the law
  - the foetus has rights from the point at which, if born, it could have a reasonable chance of survival (currently taken to be 24 weeks)
- A gradual process
  - the view of many Protestants
  - the embryo has the right to respect from conception, but full rights are acquired as the foetus develops (e.g. development of the nervous system, brain activity)

Roman Catholic views on abortion

- **Abortion** is a grave sin tantamount to murder, incurring **excommunication.**

- Human being with potential — the embryo has full rights from the start.

- Absolutely defenceless — merits special protection.

- Infinitely precious to God.

- 'When my bones were being formed...you knew that I was there — you saw me before I was born' (Psalm 139).

Young mothers can be given support by the Christian community

- All life has potential and is of equal value — not for humans to pass judgement on quality of life for a disabled foetus.

- Wrong to punish a child for his/her father's sin in case of rape — birth of child is good coming out of evil.

- The unwanted child can be adopted — brings joy to infertile couples and the chance of life and love for the child.

- Practical and emotional support given by Roman Catholic community and charities can enable young mothers to cope.

Anglican Church views on abortion

- Abortion is a great moral evil — concern about number of abortions taking place.

- In certain circumstances, abortion may be lesser of two evils, e.g. to save the mother's life and in cases of extreme distress, such as rape.

- Late abortions (i.e. after 24 weeks) for disability — only where the child would die soon after birth.

- Abortions up to 24 weeks for disability if in the child's best interests.

- Importance of compassion and love for all concerned.

- A matter for personal decision, in accordance with conscience.

Methodist Church views on abortion

- Similar to Anglican view — abortion is undesirable, but sometimes lesser of two evils.

- Justified in some cases — risk to life/health of the mother and existing family, extreme poverty, rape, severe disability.

 Case study

Joanna Jepson

- Born in 1976
- A Christian
- Had many years of operations to correct a jaw defect, for which she had suffered bullying at school
- Has a brother who has Down's Syndrome
- In 2001 she took the West Mercia police to court for not investigating the late abortion of a foetus with a cleft palate — she regarded this as unlawful killing
- Her complaint was dismissed

TopFoto

In vitro fertilisation (IVF)

IVF is a form of fertility treatment. After hormonal treatment to produce more eggs, these are removed from the woman at ovulation and fertilised with sperm (from the husband/partner or a donor) in a glass dish. The embryos are checked for viability over a few days, after which one or two are inserted into the woman's uterus, hoping for implantation. Remaining viable eggs may be frozen for future use. Any decision about their use must be a joint decision. They may be used by the couple at a future date, be donated to another couple with fertility problems, be donated for use in medical research or they may be destroyed. The **HFEA** (Human Fertilisation and Embryology Authority) regulates all use of IVF.

Protestant views on IVF

- Most Protestants see IVF as a responsible use by doctors of the skills given them by God.

- It is an act of compassion, fulfilling the command to 'love your neighbour', as infertility is a source of great and lasting distress to couples. Children are a blessing and enrich a marriage.

- It is not interfering with nature, but is putting faulty nature right.

- Many Protestants share the same concerns as Roman Catholics about the possibility of social and psychological problems arising from the use of donated sperm.

- Some, however, see sperm donation as simply another form of fertilisation and, as long as donors are not paid, as an act of love.

- The use of spare embryos for research is acceptable as they are not used after 14 days and the research is only for very serious reasons.

Roman Catholic views on IVF

- A child is a gift from God, not a right or a commodity to be ordered. **Infertility** is distressing, but there is the possibility of adoption or fostering.

- IVF separates the unitive from the procreative aspect of the sexual relationship and it also involves masturbation.

- The use of donated sperm is described as a form of 'mechanical adultery' and it may cause social and psychological problems later.

- The creation of spare embryos with the possibility of their being researched on and then destroyed disregards the **sanctity of life** and is tantamount to murder. It exploits the most defenceless of God's creatures: embryos less than 14 days old.

Key words

abortion	IVF
contraception	pro-choice
excommunication	pro-life
HFEA	sanctity of life
infertility	viability

Test yourself

Fill in each of the gaps with what you think is the correct word in the following paragraphs:

Christians believe that human life is s.............................. That means it is infinitely p.............................. and should be p...............................

Because of this, Roman Catholics think that those who have abortions are committing a very serious s............................... They are therefore e.............................. from the Church. They think that a d.............................. baby has the same right to life as anyone else and that people should not pass judgement on its q.............................. of life. They believe that if a woman who is pregnant as a result of r.............................. goes through with the pregnancy, then g.............................. has triumphed over e.............................. and the baby is not being p.............................. for what its father did.

Christians of other denominations also believe that human life is s.............................. and should be p............................... At the same time, they believe that sometimes abortion is the l.............................. of t.............................. e............................... They think this especially if the mother's l.............................. is in d.............................., if she has been r.............................. or if the baby is unlikely to l.............................. for very long because of serious d............................... In these cases, they believe that abortion may be the most c.............................. and l.............................. action to take. They think that the d.............................. is a personal one, made in accordance with c...............................

Exam tip

Ensure that you understand Christian beliefs and teachings on every topic set for study. It may help you when you are revising to have a postcard for each topic. Note down at least four beliefs or teachings relating to each of the topics.

Examination question

a Explain Roman Catholic beliefs and teachings about the use of IVF. *(4 marks)*

b Explain the views of other Christians about the use of IVF. *(4 marks)*

c 'Any action to prevent the birth of an unwanted child is the most loving thing to do.'

Do you agree? Give reasons for your answer, showing that you have thought about more than one point of view. Refer to Roman Catholic teaching in your answer. *(6 marks)*

Respect for human life — at its end

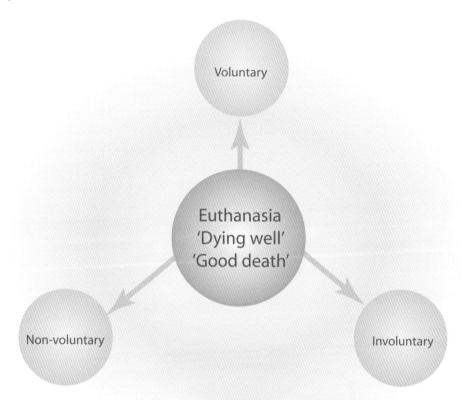

Voluntary

Euthanasia
'Dying well'
'Good death'

Non-voluntary

Involuntary

Euthanasia is often described as 'mercy killing' or 'dying with dignity'.

Voluntary euthanasia refers to the request by a person for the doctor to end a life of intolerable suffering or loss of dignity.

Non-voluntary euthanasia refers to a situation where a person is incapable of making a request, e.g. is in a long-term coma or cannot communicate at all. Euthanasia is thought to be in that individual's best interests and what he/she would have wanted.

Involuntary euthanasia refers to the kind of practice that went on in Nazi Germany, where a person is put to death without being consulted and with no thought given to the best interests of that individual.

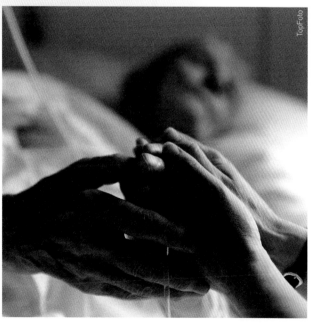

TopFoto

Making decisions about the healthcare of terminally ill patients is difficult

Euthanasia: an important distinction

Active euthanasia

May be an action taken or withheld

There is a deliberate intention to end the person's life

Illegal
The intention is to kill

Passive euthanasia

May be an action taken or withheld

The intention is to relieve suffering or to allow nature to take its course

Legal
There is no intention to kill

Some difficult questions

Active euthanasia

Can we be sure it is genuinely what the person wants? Is it a fixed and lasting desire; is it due to feelings of pressure?

Do the improvements in palliative care and the increased number of hospices make euthanasia unnecessary?

What about removing feeding tubes from persistent vegitative state (PVS) patients? Are those tubes medical treatment or are they a part of basic care to which everyone has an absolute right?

Passive euthanasia

Can we be sure of intentions? Is giving a high dose of morphine to a cancer patient intended only to relieve pain, or might it be also to end the person's life more quickly?

Does withholding or withdrawing treatment from a dying person just prolong the suffering?

Suicide is not illegal. So is it an act of discrimination not to allow those incapable of ending their lives themselves to have help in doing so from their doctors?

Dignity in Dying

Campaigns to legalise:

- voluntary euthanasia
- **living wills**

The ProLife Alliance

Campaigns to promote:

- the right to life as fundamental
- the provision of more hospices

Hospices

Hospices provide highly skilled and individual care for the terminally and incurably ill. They specialise in **palliative care** and many offer a wide variety of treatments to make it possible for patients to have the best possible quality of life in the final weeks or months of their lives. They aim at allowing patients to die with dignity. The needs of relatives are also taken into account. They are included in the preparation for death and their pain is eased. Most hospices are for adults, but there are an increasing number of children's and teenagers' hospices.

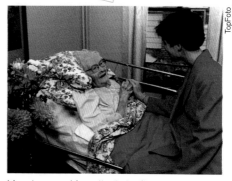

Hospices enable patients to die with dignity

Roman Catholic views on euthanasia

- Totally opposed to all forms of active euthanasia.

- God gave life and only he has the right to take it: euthanasia is 'playing God'.

- The body is a 'temple of the Holy Spirit' and so is sacred (1 Corinthians 6:19).

- It breaks the fifth commandment: do not commit murder.

- God's gift of the power of responsible decision-making has limits: it does not include taking one's own life as that is not responsible stewardship.

- It shows a lack of trust in God's love, compassion and mercy.

- It makes judgements about someone's value and quality of life that are not for humans to make: in God's eyes all humans are of equal value, whatever their circumstances.

- It deprives vulnerable people of protection from abuse and from the slippery slope that might permit first voluntary, then non-voluntary and maybe, ultimately, involuntary euthanasia.

NB These views are also held by all mainstream Christian denominations, e.g. the Anglican Church.

Views of some individual Christians

- Life is sacred and should normally be preserved, but not at all costs.

- Quality of life is more important than biological existence.

- God would not want people to undergo intolerable suffering or complete loss of dignity — this is not what it means to be 'in God's image'.

- The decision for euthanasia may be an act of responsible decision-making and a way of enabling God's will for the individual to be done.

- Euthanasia may be the most compassionate option, especially in those cases where pain cannot be relieved and where the person is totally dependent for everything on others.

- Death is easier to come to terms with and face if the fear of intolerable suffering is removed.

NB Although the mainstream denominations are all opposed to it, many individuals within those churches support the legalising of voluntary euthanasia, and some individual Church leaders support it.

Case study

Lilian Boyes and Dr Nigel Cox

- Lilian Boyes suffered from rheumatoid arthritis

- Her consultant was Dr Nigel Cox

- In 1991 she was admitted to hospital

- She was always in extreme pain and could not bear anyone to touch her or hold her hand

- She repeatedly asked Dr Cox to give her a lethal injection

- Eventually, out of compassion, he gave her an injection of potassium chloride, which was not a painkiller but would stop her heart

- He entered this in the hospital notes and it was when these were later checked that he was reported for his action

- In 1992 he was convicted of attempted murder, but was given a suspended prison sentence

- He was allowed to continue to practise medicine

Key words

active euthanasia

euthanasia

hospices

involuntary euthanasia

living wills

non-voluntary euthanasia

palliative care

passive euthanasia

voluntary euthanasia

Test yourself

True or false?

	TRUE	FALSE
Voluntary euthanasia is illegal but non-voluntary euthanasia is legal in the UK.	☐	☐
Active euthanasia is illegal but passive euthanasia is legal in the UK.	☐	☐
Giving a cancer patient morphine to relieve pain, even though it will shorten the person's life, is allowed in UK law.	☐	☐
The Anglican Church agrees with voluntary euthanasia.	☐	☐
The Roman Catholic Church agrees with voluntary euthanasia.	☐	☐
Hospices are homes for the elderly.	☐	☐
Hospices specialise in palliative care.	☐	☐
There are hospices for children.	☐	☐
Dignity in Dying is an organisation that opposes legalising voluntary euthanasia.	☐	☐
The ProLife Alliance opposes legalising voluntary euthanasia.	☐	☐

Examination question

a Explain how belief in the sanctity of life might influence a Christian's attitude to voluntary euthanasia. *(4 marks)*

b 'When people are suffering unbearable pain, voluntary euthanasia is the kindest action to take.'

Do you agree? Give reasons for your answer, showing that you have thought about more than one point of view. Refer to Roman Catholic teaching in your answer. *(6 marks)*

Exam tip

When answering a 6-mark evaluation question, remember that to reach more than level 3 you need to include relevant reference to Roman Catholic or Christian teaching.

The question will indicate whether specifically Roman Catholic or more general Christian teaching is required.

Christian responses to global issues

Vocation in action

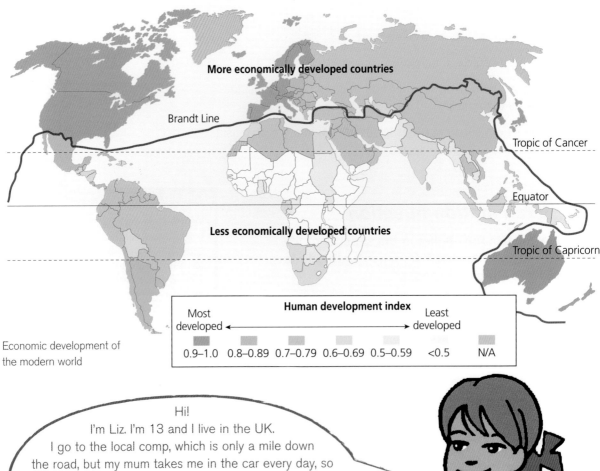

More economically developed countries

Brandt Line

Tropic of Cancer

Equator

Less economically developed countries

Tropic of Capricorn

Economic development of the modern world

Human development index

Most developed ← → Least developed

0.9–1.0   0.8–0.89   0.7–0.79   0.6–0.69   0.5–0.59   <0.5   N/A

Hi!
I'm Liz. I'm 13 and I live in the UK.
I go to the local comp, which is only a mile down
the road, but my mum takes me in the car every day, so
I don't have to get up early. I love weekends, as then I go
down to town with my friends — we sometimes buy DVDs
or clothes if our mums are feeling generous, and we
always go for a burger. I hope to go to uni and
then work in a big law firm.

Hi! I'm Grace. I'm 13 and I live in Uganda. My parents both died of AIDS when I was little and I hardly remember them. Luckily, my aunt said she would look after me even though she's a widow, so I live with her and my three young cousins. But we don't have enough money for me to go to school so I help her with the animals. I also fetch water and sometimes prepare the meal that we have once a day. I'd love to become a teacher, but that is just a dream — I can't read or write.

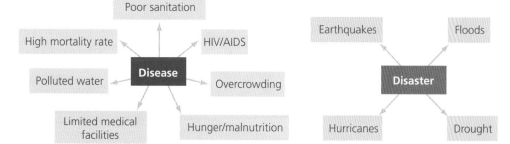

Characteristics of less developed countries

Response to global poverty

A small percentage of the UK's national income is given annually to projects in less economically developed countries (LEDCs) to help reduce poverty. In an emergency, e.g. the 2004 Asian tsunami, large sums are given for immediate relief. But much of the response comes from charities.

Types of aid given to poor countries	
Emergency aid	**Long-term aid**
Aid given in the short term to help people survive in a crisis	Aid given over a few years to fund projects aimed at enabling self-reliance

 Case study

CAFOD

- Began with first Family Fast Day in 1960, organised by National Board of Catholic Women
- Set up by Catholic Bishops of England and Wales in 1962 as official overseas development and relief agency
- Works with over 500 partners in the UK and overseas
- Also works with other UK agencies, e.g. Disasters Emergency Committee and with interfaith groups, e.g. Islamic Relief
- Helped to set up **Fair trade** movement
- Basic principles — compassion, solidarity, **stewardship**, hope
- Concerned to promote human development and social justice
- Involved in emergency and long-term aid, in encouraging a more simple lifestyle in the UK and in speaking out against injustice

Cafod activists lobbying parliament to make poverty history

Case study

Trócaire

- Set up by the Irish Catholic bishops in 1973 as the official overseas development agency of the Catholic Church in Ireland
- Means 'mercy' in English
- Works in 39 countries across Asia, Africa, Latin America and the Middle East
- Stresses the dignity, fundamental human rights and responsibilities of all people, regardless of race, creed, culture
- Raises awareness of root causes of poverty and injustice and encourages action
- Involved in emergency and long-term aid

Fair trade

This movement was started by a number of aid agencies and organisations. Fair trade aims at removing the injustice at the heart of much world trade, e.g. those who work on banana plantations for multinational companies are very poorly paid. Fair trade aims to give the producers of goods a fair wage for their goods. Those involved in the movement also aim to provide decent living and working conditions for the workers, including schools for children and medical care. They encourage the setting up of cooperatives and the use of suitable technology.

This logo appears on all Fairtrade produce

Christian attitudes to world poverty

- All mainstream Christian denominations take an active part in working towards ending global poverty.
- They emphasise:
  - justice
  - stewardship
  - compassion
  - following the example of Jesus
- They follow New Testament teaching that it is not enough to say that poverty is wrong; action is needed, and a person who ignores someone in need cannot possibly claim to love God (1 John 3:17–18).
- Christians are called to give generously and self-sacrificially of their money, their time and their talents.
- The Roman Catholic Church teaches that rich nations have a moral duty to help poor nations, both by giving direct aid and by reforming those international agencies (e.g. the World Trade Organization) that keep poor nations poor.
- Many Christians give up luxuries in Lent, take part in fast days, Lenten lunches, and in sponsored activities.
- Many also take part in campaigns such as Make Poverty History.

The parable of the sheep and the goats: Matthew 25:31–46

Jesus told this parable to show that, when he returned on Judgement Day, all people, whatever their race, would be judged according to how they treated other people.

He would divide everyone into two groups, just as a Palestinian shepherd separates his flock of sheep and goats at night time. He would welcome those on his right to God's presence, saying that when he was hungry, thirsty, cold, naked, sick or in prison, they had come to his aid. When they queried this, he said: 'Whatever you did for others, however low their status might be, you did for me.'

Those on his left were to be excluded from God's presence, for they had failed to help others, and in doing so, they had failed to help him.

Key words

CAFOD	stewardship
emergency aid	Trócaire
Fair trade	
long-term aid	

Exam tip

In this course, there are a number of biblical passages set for study. You must learn these in detail and understand how they might be applied to the topic to which they are attached. You may be asked questions on these passages in the examination.

Test yourself

1 Give six facts about CAFOD or Trócaire in the chart below:

CAFOD or Trócaire

2 Match up the two columns in the chart on the parable of the sheep and the goats:

I was hungry		You clothed me
I was thirsty		You did it for me
I was cold		You visited me
I was naked		You visited me
I was ill		You gave me a drink
I was in prison		You gave me shelter
Whatever you did for even the least important person		You fed me

Examination question

a Retell Jesus' parable of the sheep and the goats. *(6 marks)*

Do you like my new skirt and top? I went to that big store on the high street and I was really lucky. My mum gave me some money to treat myself, and because they were so cheap, I had enough to go and buy some earrings that I've been wanting for ages. I really couldn't believe how cheap they were — I got a real bargain. And they were made in India — so I feel as if I've been helping the poor.

You must be joking. That store was on the news last week — an undercover reporter had discovered that those who make clothes for it are really exploited — they work long hours in awful conditions for almost nothing. If you really want to help the poor, be more careful where you shop.

b Explain briefly how the Fair trade movement seeks to help workers in poor nations. *(3 marks)*

c 'If people have poor working conditions, their own governments should sort it out. It's not our concern.'

Do you agree? Give reasons for your answer, showing that you have thought about more than one point of view. Refer to Christian teaching in your answer. *(6 marks)*

War and peace

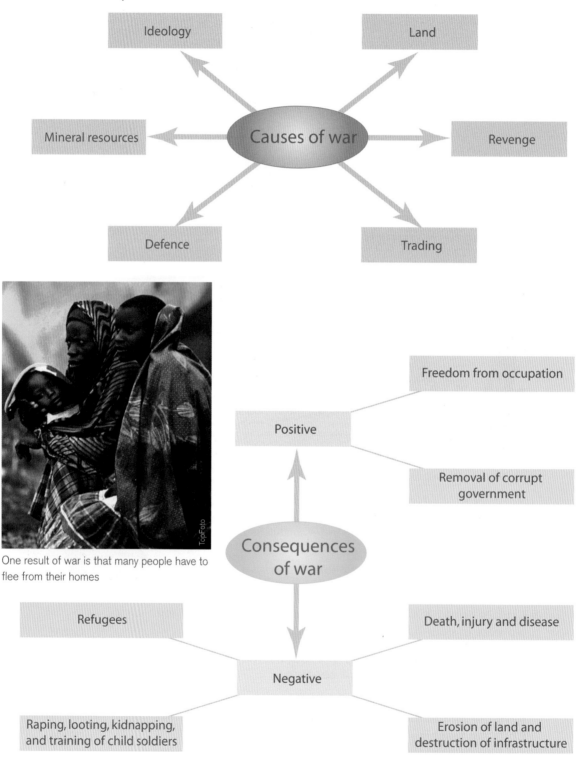

Causes of war
- Ideology
- Land
- Mineral resources
- Revenge
- Defence
- Trading

One result of war is that many people have to flee from their homes

TopFoto

Consequences of war

Positive
- Freedom from occupation
- Removal of corrupt government

Negative
- Refugees
- Death, injury and disease
- Raping, looting, kidnapping, and training of child soldiers
- Erosion of land and destruction of infrastructure

Types of warfare

Conventional warfare covers a wide range of weaponry, including:

■ atomic (nuclear)
■ biological
■ chemical

The first example of **nuclear warfare** was in August 1945 when the USA dropped atomic bombs on Hiroshima and Nagasaki in Japan. Thousands died immediately and many more thousands died slowly from the effects of radiation. Still today, people are dying of cancers related to the dropping of those bombs.

Many nations, including the UK, have nuclear weapons. They see them as a deterrent: possessing them protects them from attack. Some other nations are in the process of developing nuclear technology, which is a cause of concern. **Nuclear proliferation** might lead to irresponsible leaders or terrorists getting hold of such weapons and using them.

Many people want to see a reduction in the numbers of weapons. There are two approaches:

■ **Multilateral disarmament**
   – reduction by international treaties
■ **Unilateral disarmament**
   – a nation getting rid of its weapons irrespective of the actions of other nations
   – CND campaigns for unilateral disarmament

The atomic bomb dropped on Hiroshima completely destroyed the city

Protesters campaigning for nuclear disarmament

Terrorism

This is the often indiscriminate use of violence to achieve particular political or religious goals, to redress injustice or to overthrow a regime. Whatever the motive, **terrorism** is aimed at creating an atmosphere of fear and putting pressure on those in power. A common form of terrorism is suicide bombing, and those who die in this way are regarded as martyrs. Terrorists justify their actions as a last resort: they see them as the only way of making people listen to their grievances. Most people, however, condemn all acts of terrorism, claiming that they show a total disregard for life and can never be justified.

The Just War theory

The **Just War Theory** refers to the belief that war is never a good thing, but may sometimes be justified as the lesser of two evils. It is a very ancient theory, but was developed over the centuries by great thinkers in the Roman Catholic Church. Some politicians and journalists use it when assessing whether or not conflict is justified. For a war to be declared just, eight criteria are taken into account.

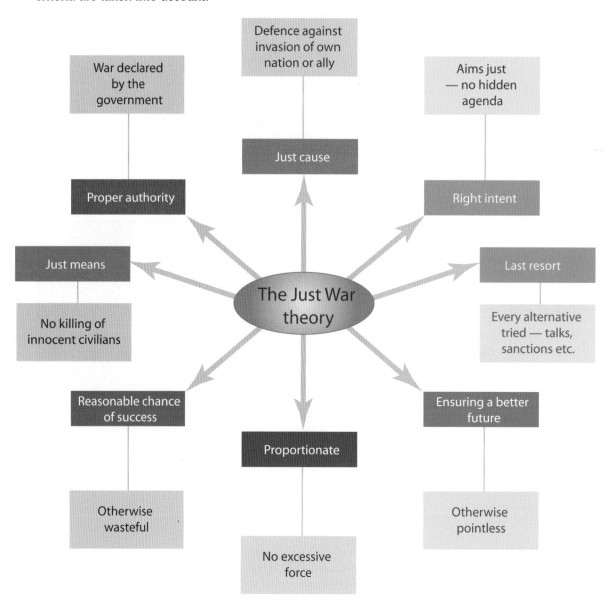

Pacifism

This is the belief that violence against other human beings can never be justified. War is always wrong — it can never be the lesser of two evils. There are strong arguments both for and against **pacifism**.

Arguments for pacifism	Arguments against pacifism
Beliefs about human life ■ everyone has the right to life ■ life is sacred ■ lives should be treated with respect ■ all are brothers and sisters	**The right to life is not absolute** ■ an aggressor has forfeited that right by the act of aggression ■ some lives may be sacrificed to protect others
War causes immense suffering ■ modern methods in particular harm the innocent ■ the suffering caused is out of all proportion to the evil being fought ■ the emotional suffering may affect future generations	**The Just War conditions** ■ seek to protect the innocent ■ ensure proportionality in violence ■ refusal to fight may make aggressors think they can do whatever they want, which may result in more suffering. It is important to defend and protect the innocent and sometimes this can be done only through war
War is a waste of resources ■ the money spent in the UK on weapons would solve social and global problems ■ money should be spent on saving lives, not destroying them ■ it causes irreparable damage to the environment ■ it uses up minerals and other resources	**War can be a wise use of resources** ■ wars that are fought to end injustice may save money and resources in the long run as greedy oppressors waste resources even more
War encourages undesirable attitudes ■ e.g. greed, hatred, prejudice, lust for power, arrogance	**War brings out the best in people** ■ e.g. courage, comradeship, compassion, humility, desire for justice

Christian attitudes to war and peace

■ The different views of Christians do not coincide with differences in denominations, i.e. some Roman Catholics, Anglicans and Methodists are pacifist and some are not.

■ The Society of Friends (Quakers) is the only denomination that is officially pacifist.

■ There are many Christian pacifist groups, e.g. Pax Christi.

■ Christian pacifists refer to the teaching of Jesus:
  – love your enemies and pray for your persecutors
  – those who live by the sword die by the sword

■ Christians who are not pacifist tend to agree with the approach of the Just War theory.

■ They claim that the teaching and example of Jesus were unrelated to issues of war and peace and should not be taken literally or distorted.

■ St Paul told Christians to obey rulers because they were given their authority from God.

■ The Catechism of the Roman Catholic Church supports the Just War theory, accepting that war may occasionally be a 'necessary evil'.

■ Pope John XXIII spoke out against nuclear weapons in 1963.

■ Terrorism is denounced by Christians as totally against the teaching of Jesus, e.g. to love one's enemies.

Dietrich Bonhoeffer

Statue of Dietrich Bonhoeffer who was commemorated as a martyr, Westminster Abbey

- Born in Germany in 1906
- Protestant Christian
- Studied theology and became a Lutheran pastor
- Co-founded the Confessing Church — which opposed Hitler and the Nazis
- Helped Jews escape from Germany
- Rejected earlier pacifist views because he believed that the evil of Nazism could be overcome only by violence
- Plotted overthrow of Hitler
- Arrested and eventually moved to Flossenburg concentration camp
- Hanged in April 1945
- Commemorated as a martyr by the Church of England

Key words

Just War theory
multilateral disarmament
nuclear proliferation
nuclear warfare
pacifism
terrorism
unilateral disarmament

Test yourself

1 Read through the following statements relating to the Second World War. Next to each, say which criterion of the Just War theory could be applied and then put a tick or cross, indicating whether you think it was fulfilled or not. The first has been done for you as an example:

The UK went to war with Germany because Hitler invaded Poland, with whom the UK had an alliance	*Just cause*	✓
The British government declared war on Germany		
Before declaring war, Britain had held talks with Hitler and made a treaty, but Hitler ignored it		
Britain had an army, a navy and an air force that were reasonably equipped		
Europe suffered terribly under Nazi rule. After the war, Eastern Europe was dominated by the Soviet Union and its repressive policies		
Thousands of civilians died in the bombing of Dresden by the RAF and allies		
The Americans dropped nuclear bombs on Hiroshima and Nagasaki		
When Germany surrendered, the British and Americans began to help German refugees		

2 Give three reasons why pacifists did not agree with the UK going to war against Germany in 1939.

3 Explain briefly two consequences of war.

Examination question

a 'Christians who fight in a war are betraying their faith.'
   What do you think? Explain your opinion. (3 marks)

b Explain why many Christians are pacifists. (6 marks)

c Explain why many Christians support the Just War theory. (6 marks)

Exam tip
When explaining views, you may find it helpful in developing your answer to give examples of people or organisations that hold those views.

Key word index